EXPLORING
BUSINESS
AND
ECONOMICS

EXPLORING
BUSINESS
AND
ECONOMICS

The
Economy

Terence O'Hara

Chelsea House Publishers
Philadelphia

Frontis: Space Shuttle Endeavor launches from the Kennedy Space Center. American tax dollars help fund expensive federal projects like the space program.

CHELSEA HOUSE PUBLISHERS

EDITOR-IN-CHIEF Sally Cheney
DIRECTOR OF PRODUCTION Kim Shinners
PRODUCTION MANAGER Pamela Loos
ART DIRECTOR Sara Davis

Choptank Syndicate/Chestnut Productions

EDITORIAL Norman Macht and Mary Hull
PRODUCTION Lisa Hochstein
PICTURE RESEARCH Norman Macht

http://www.chelseahouse.com

First Printing

1 3 5 7 9 8 6 4 2

Library of Congress Cataloging-in-Publication Data

O'Hara, Terence.
    The economy / Terence O'Hara
    p. cm. – (Exploring business and economics)
    ISBN 0-7910-6641-X (alk. paper)
1. Economics. I. Title. II. Series.
HB71 .O35 2001
330—dc21   2001042508

Table of Contents

NEW
Gotta catch all
6 boxes

KRAFT

Macaroni & Cheese

D I N N E R

POKÉMON™

•PIKACHU•
1 OF 6

NET WT
5.5 OZ (155g)

A popular macaroni and cheese brand teamed up with the creators of Pokémon, a popular cartoon character, to market a series of collectible boxes that kids would ask their parents to buy for them.

Land of Opportunity

Think back to all the things that you did getting ready for school this morning. Maybe you used a toothbrush, watched TV, or ate cereal for breakfast? On the way to school, did you see billboards with advertisements or buy something at the grocery or convenience store?

In some ways, all these things have to do with business and the free market **economy** that exists in the United States today. In a **free market**, anyone can think up an idea for a product and try to sell it. And, boy, do Americans think up new products and sell them. The United States bought and sold nine trillion dollars worth of stuff last year. That's a lot of toothpaste, video games, CDs, and cereals. For example, Americans buy $8 billion worth of breakfast cereal every year. Kellogg, which makes cereal brands such as Fruit Loops and Corn Flakes, earns about 30 percent of that total. As a whole, the American breakfast cereal industry spends more than $700 million a year buying advertising.

For Americans, the huge amount of money we spend and the wide variety of products we can buy are the result of this country's long association with the ideals of liberty, private property, and the free market. Thought of in that way, your Cheerios are a result of our free market, democratic ideals. But the man who invented Cheerios, James Ford Bell—who made a fortune in flour and cereal after he bought up several grain mills in the 1920s to form the General Mills Company—probably wasn't thinking politically. All he wanted to do was make a buck. And for most of the history of the United States, it has been a great place to do that.

The United States has grown fast, expanding in both population and geographic area several fold by 1900.

Richest Americans as of 2001

1. WILLIAM H. GATES, Seattle, Washington. *Net worth: $63 billion*

2. LAWRENCE ELLISON, Atherton, California. *Net worth: $58 billion*

3. PAUL ALLEN, Seattle, Washington. *Net worth: $36 billion*

4. WARREN BUFFET, Omaha, Nebraska. *Net worth $28 billion*

5. GORDON MOORE, Woodside, California. *Net worth: $26 billion*

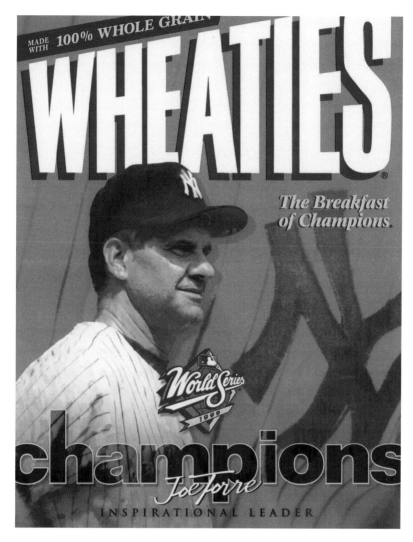

New products come and go all the time on supermarket shelves. One way to help sell a product is to put a popular sports star on the packaging.

According to the U.S. Census Bureau, there are now more than 281 million people living in the United States. And the U.S. population grew more between 1990 and 2000 than it has during any 10-year period in American history. This 32.7 million jump even beats the explosive "baby boom"

A basic crop, corn can be used for eating, animal feed, cooking oil, or fuel. In 1800, when America was a nation of small farmers like these, it took five farm workers to feed one citizen. Today, with large scale farming and modern machinery, one farm worker can produce enough to feed 200 people.

population growth of 28 million between 1950 and 1960. Populations booms are good for business. All these people mean that there are a lot of consumers to buy the goods and services that people put up for sale.

For much of the 20th century, America expanded its business interests at home, developing a strong domestic economy. After World War II the United States expanded its business interests abroad, exporting goods to other parts of the world. The United States became the richest country in the world after World War II.

Today, four of the six richest people in the world are Americans. Bill Gates, who owns most of Microsoft—the company that makes your school or home computers work—is worth tens of billions of dollars all by himself. He lives in Seattle, Washington. And, though for every big winner there are always several people who don't do so well and several who end up poor, America still has one of the highest **standards of living** of any country in the world.

That means most people here have enough money in their pockets to keep a roof over their head, the heater going, and food on their table. And it's one reason so many people and families—hundreds of thousands of them—from around the world move to the United States from other countries every year.

Though you might not realize it, you are a major piece of America's economy. The decisions you make on how to spend or save some of your money are the basis for everything that happens in our free market system.

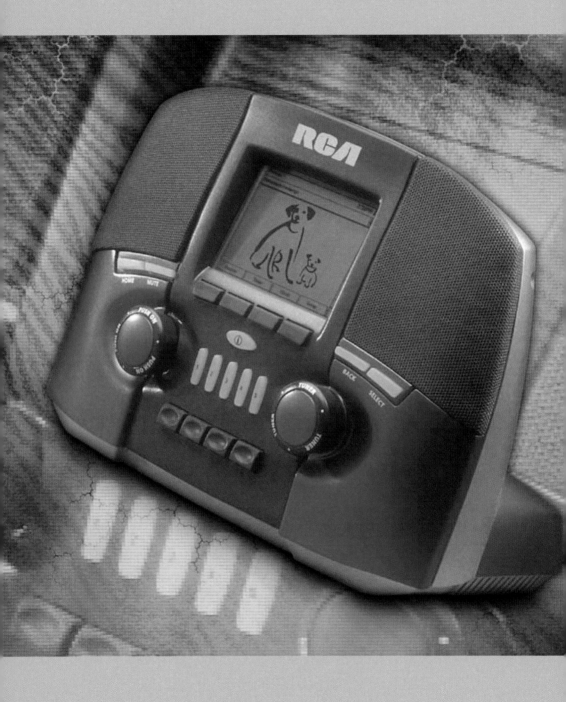

The Internet has led to all kinds of new products. This RCA radio uses an Ethernet connection to tap into the Internet, allowing the listener to tune in to thousands of radio stations.

Free Enterprise

A free enterprise system means that people are free to risk their own money or property to create more of both. This is a fundamental principle of a free market economy.

In a free market economy, each individual is allowed to own property—a house, a car, an office building, a business—and do with it whatever he or she pleases, within the limits of the law. In theory, each person in this economic system is in constant competition with everyone else for more property. This may sound like the "law of the jungle" in which every individual is out for him or herself, but it pretty much sums up the idea behind a free market system.

When it works, the system is designed to create wealth, ease the transfer of knowledge, encourage a system of laws that everyone lives by, and increase the overall well-being of the people that live under it. In a free market system, which some people call **capitalism,** everyone is free to work out as best a life as they can make, using their own skills, talent and property. This usually means that people have to take risks.

Have you ever run a foot race against one of your friends? Sometimes the reward for winning is money, but usually it's just to find out who can run faster. But by deciding to run the race, you automatically take the chance of losing it. That is risk, and it is what every businessperson goes through every day when deciding how best to make money. For a free market system to work, every businessperson has to be free to take risks. Some lose, some win. It's the competition that matters in a free market, not the outcome.

There is an old saying, "Nothing ventured, nothing gained." This is true of a businessperson in a capitalist economy.

The Inventor of Corn Flakes

Will Keith Kellogg worked as a clerk at the Battle Creek Sanitarium in Battle Creek, Michigan. It was there, searching for a vegetarian diet for patients, that he discovered cereal flakes. That's how Corn Flakes were invented. Even though he never went past sixth grade in school, Kellogg built a fortune by selling cereals like Corn Flakes, Frosted Flakes, and Rice Krispies. He built the biggest cereal company in the world and was one of America's great charitable givers. He died in 1951 at the age of 91.

On October 18, 1892, Alexander Graham Bell launched the long distance telephone line between New York and Chicago. Inventions like the telephone enabled the national economy to grow much faster in the 20th century than it had previously.

Consider James Ford Bell, who founded the General Mills Company that makes such breakfast cereals as Cheerios and Kix. In the 1920s, Bell already had a thriving business in Minnesota grinding up wheat for flour. But he risked his fortune by borrowing money to buy up a bunch of other flour mills in the Midwest. For Bell to succeed, flour prices would have to stay high enough for him to make a profit on his business expansion, and people would have to keep on buying his brand of baking mix, which he called Bisquick. But what if flour prices fell or Bell's competitors sold better, cheaper flour? If that happened, Bell could lose it

Not every new gadget made its inventors rich and famous. In the 1920s these two men invented a device to drop air mail sacks from airplanes so the pilot wouldn't have to land to deliver the mail. They didn't sell many.

all. He took the risk, and he won, and today the company he founded sells Cheerios, Wheaties, and a variety of other foods you see in the grocery store every day.

To be sure, Bell's competitors didn't lie down and let their Corn Flakes get mushy. Will Kellogg was Bell's main competition, and they fought each other on the supermarket shelves for decades. The companies they founded are still competitors today. They compete on innovation—the creation of new and interesting products that people don't even know they want yet. They compete on price (count how many of the coupons in the Sunday paper are for cereal). And they compete by creating demand for their particular brand of breakfast cereal, usually through advertising on television. The next time you watch cartoons on Saturday morning, notice how many breakfast cereal commercials there are.

Through all these things, individuals and companies take risks and hope to end up with more money than they had when they started. In the case of both Bell and Kellogg, they became two of the richest men in America. Even with all that competition, they were both winners.

Do you know who George R. Stibitz, Douglas Engelbart, Edwin Armstrong, and Philo Farnsworth are? None is famous, though each is responsible in his own way for much of the electronics that surround you every day. George R. Stibitz invented the modern computer, Douglas Engelbart invented the computer mouse, Edwin Armstrong invented FM radio, and Philo Farnsworth invented television.

Upon each man's invention a huge industry was built that changed the world. Each man was a scientist first, and not that interested in making a lot of money, though most of them did. And each man invented or thought up all kinds of interesting ideas and inventions that didn't make a lot of money, too. But business, when it is left to its own devices, has a way of finding inventions that have the most money-making potential and making the most of them.

Business and the free market economy are probably at their best and most exciting when they help fund and commercialize inventions that can change people's lives. If the American economy is good at one thing, it is encouraging inventions and finding new ways to build, sell, and use them.

Innovation is the process by which new ideas are developed, and it is how new and better ways of doing things are accomplished. This freedom to tinker and experiment is an important strength of the free market system, and without it the economy would grow stale.

One of America's great examples of innovation in business was the Ford Motor Company, which was founded by Henry Ford in the early 20th century. Henry Ford wasn't a great thinker. In fact, a lot of his contemporaries thought he was a bully. He didn't even invent the automobile. But Henry Ford almost single-handedly invented modern manufacturing. The way he made his cars changed the entire business world and the world economy.

Henry Ford was a farmer's son from Dearborn, Michigan, who left home to work as a machinist in Detroit. In 1903, he formed the Ford Motor Company. Five years later, he invented and began producing the Model T, a cheap, durable car that, more than any other product, turned Americans into the car-crazy people they are today. By 1918, half of all cars on the road were Model Ts.

Henry Ford and his car company were already well established and very successful by 1910, when he opened a huge production facility in Highland Park, Michigan. It

A Nation of Inventors

Americans are an inventive people. In this country the government grants patents to anyone who comes up with a unique product or idea. Patents are a kind of legal protection, allowing inventors to own their own ideas. It's a great way to make sure that the men and women who invent things actually profit from their inventions, and that their inventions are not stolen. In 1999 more than 288,000 applications were made for patents; 169,000 of them were granted.

New inventions fuel growing economies, and Thomas Edison came up with more of them than just about anybody. Phonographs like this one built into a doll, light bulbs, stock tickers, batteries, cement mixers, and synthetic shoe rubber are some of the things that flowed from his fertile mind.

was here, between 1910 and 1913, that Ford revolutionized manufacturing. Before Ford came along, automobiles were very expensive to manufacture because they took a lot of time to make. But Ford changed all that. He combined precision manufacturing with the use of standardized and interchangeable parts, so that each automobile would have the same size parts and the parts of any one car could be used in any other. Ford also divided the labor of his workers into specialized areas. In 1913, this division of labor resulted in the creation of a moving assembly line. Workers stayed in one place and added one part at a time as the car moved past them. Parts were delivered to every worker on conveyor belts. More than anything, the assembly line made it very cheap to make a lot of cars, and it made Ford Motor the biggest car manufacturer in the world.

Today, there are a lot of examples of companies that, like Ford Motor, have changed the world. Bill Gates, the founder of Microsoft, believed that the software that made computers run would really be what people wanted. Today, most personal computers are alike, no matter what brand. But almost every computer has to use Microsoft software. That has made Bill Gates the richest man in the world.

Innovations are making lots of money and changing the world every day. The best recent example is the **Internet,** which was created by a group of government workers and college professors in 1983. The Internet, a network of computers that allows information to be shared around the world and brought into the privacy of one's own home, has revolutionized the way many companies do business. Today the Internet is everywhere, and is one of the main reasons why people use computers at all. The Internet is used for learning, entertainment, and buying and selling things. Like Ford's assembly line, the Internet is so innovative that it is changing a lot of different industries that never knew the Internet existed 10 years ago.

The Internet provides a whole new way to market products. It can connect a distant buyer with a seller, bypassing a middleman. It has also enabled some workers to "telecommute"—to work from home via a computer with a modem instead of driving into the office. The Internet also enables research scientists to communicate with other researchers and share the results of their work online, leading to increased collaboration.

No one is certain where the Internet will take us, but many business experts believe the Internet will one day make it unnecessary to read a newspaper, or watch TV, or buy music. Henry Ford and his assembly line made every other kind of manufacturing out of date, and the Internet could make every other kind of information sharing out of date, too.

There are 30 major league baseball teams and very few players who can hit and play shortstop like Alex Rodriguez. If the supply of "A-Rods" equaled the demand, the Texas Rangers would not have signed him to the richest contract in baseball history.

The Law of Supply and Demand

Sometimes people do crazy things, and spend a lot of money on something they desperately need or want, that a lot of other people need or want just as much. This is the underlying principle of **supply and demand:** if more people want something, and there is a limited supply of it, its cost goes up.

In 2000 the Sony Corporation came out with Play Station 2, the hottest home video gaming system ever. If you could find it in a store, it cost anywhere between $100 and $200. The problem was you couldn't find it in a store. Demand was so high for Play Station 2 that stores ran out of them. But the demand for new game machines didn't go away just because the supply

Hoping to purchase a Sony Play Station 2 video game console, over 100 people waited in line for two hours at a store in Topeka, Kansas, on October 26, 2000. Sony had warned that a parts shortage would limit its initial shipment of the much-anticipated entertainment system.

was limited. So the cost went through the roof. A market for the games was created that didn't include stores at all. Instead, individuals sold them on Internet commerce sites. On the Internet, Play Station 2 owners were offering them for sale for thousands of dollars. And people paid it. Why? Because there was a limited supply, and the demand for the game was very high. That usually means high prices.

If Sony had made a lot more Play Stations than there were people who wanted to buy them, the price would have dropped. This happens to many toys and gift items after the annual holiday season. Once Christmas is past, the demand for gifts drops off significantly, and so do prices. The result: after-Christmas sales. What this means is that a smart business person, or entrepreneur, who buys something when demand is low, and sells it when demand is high, can earn a lot of money.

Here's another example of supply and demand driving up prices: Alex Rodriguez signed a contract with the Texas Rangers baseball club to play shortstop, a deal that will pay Rodriguez $252 million over 10 years. That's $25 million a year, the most expensive major league baseball contract ever.

A lot of things went into the decision to pay Rodriguez that much money, but it all boiled down to this: the Texas Rangers make a lot of money from television and from selling the team's logo. There's only one Alex Rodriguez, and fans like him. That translates into television viewers and

Weighing Costs and Benefits

There are no free lunches. An economist once used that sentence to describe a basic law of economics: everything, even if you think it's free, costs something. And cost in this way doesn't mean just money. There can be all kinds of costs. This idea of cost helps explain a lot of things about economics. It's never an exact science, but more a series of common sense notions that help explain why people act the way they do. To an economist, every decision a person makes is rooted in a cost-benefit analysis: in other words, what will it cost me and what will I get out of it? "Should I get up out of this chair to sharpen my pencil? If I do, I might interrupt the teacher, who would become upset with me. But a sharper pencil would make my writing neater. What do I do?" This example is, in a simple form, what goes through most people's heads when they decide to do anything.

people who will buy Texas Rangers hats, which means more income for the Texas Rangers.

Of course, it is still a big risk for the Rangers. What if Rodriguez gets injured and can't play baseball, or a new ultra-star shortstop shows up, and he plays for the Houston Astros? A lot of things can happen to make the whole thing a flop or a huge success, but the Rangers still took the risk.

Supply and demand happens in much less noticeable ways, of course, but it determines the cost of everything you buy and some things you don't buy. For example, if you trade baseball cards, or Pokémons, you know that to acquire a hard-to-find card you may have to exchange a lot of different cards for just one card. That is supply and demand at work, and for the businessman it's a powerful tool for making money, or losing a lot of it.

Tulip Mania

In the 1600s in Denmark, people were crazy for tulips, so much so that the demand for rare or unique tulips hit fever pitches and drove the price of tulip bulbs—the onion-like roots of tulips—to incredible heights. By 1635 much of the Dutch economy was tied to the ever-rising prices of tulip bulbs. Both the rich and poor threw their fortunes at tulip bulbs, with most never even planting them but hoping to sell them again at a quick profit. The prices reached today's equivalent of hundreds of thousands of dollars a bulb. But the market couldn't sustain itself, and in 1636 the market crashed and the Dutch economy took years to recover. People lost everything betting that demand for tulip bulbs would keep increasing. The phenomenon became known as Tulip Mania, and is often used to describe any trend that goes beyond all reason.

A shopper looks at nearly empty shelves in a Scarsdale, New York super-market, hoping to stock up on food in preparation for a winter storm. Store shelves empty rapidly when storms or hurricanes are predicted.

By the way, the most money ever paid for a baseball card was $1.27 million. The card, sold at auction in the summer of 2000, was a rare 1909 card of Honus Wagner, who was a shortstop for the Pittsburgh Pirates. You can bet there aren't many Honus Wagner baseball cards around if that one sold for over a million. This is the principle of supply and demand at work.

The American economy is not built entirely of giant corporations and shopping malls. Small businesses like this second-hand plumbing supply store are the heart of the American free enterprise system, where anyone can go into business for himself.

How Businesses Work

How does business get done? Well, the easy answer is that business—the millions of transactions a day that make up a free market economy—is made up of people like you and your family. But in order to get the business done, structures need to be put into place that help people exchange goods and services.

Businesses come in all shapes and sizes. Sometimes a business is just one person, an independent contractor or consultant who sells his or her skills or talent. Most often, however, businesses are corporations made up of many people, typically the owners, the managers, and the workers.

The start of the industrial age took many people off the farms and into offices and factories. Hundreds of people now sat in huge offices all day operating business machines like these calculators. This was considered a good job in the early 1900s.

Business owners risk their own **capital.** That means that if the company loses money, the owners personally lose money. If the company loses so much money that it goes out of business or files for bankruptcy, the owners can lose everything they invested in the business.

It's the owner's job to hire the managers. Managers are usually paid by the owners (although sometimes managers also own the business) to make the business profitable. They hire and fire the workers, help develop a strategy for the business, and take responsibility for making sure things get done. The most obvious example of a manager is the CEO, the chief executive officer, the boss. CEO pay has been going up dramatically in the last 10 years, and many

Offices have changed a lot in the last 100 years, but their function has not: they are still places where business is conducted.

successful CEOs become super-rich in their own right, even though they may not own more than a small part of the companies they run. The average pay of CEOs of America's biggest companies was $10.6 million a year in 1998. The average annual pay of a production worker was $22,976.

Workers are paid a **wage** to do the everyday work of the business. Workers make cars for automobile makers, they sell washing machines for Maytag, and they add and subtract numbers for accounting companies. Historically, workers have not had the opportunity or the money to own what they make.

Labor unions, organizations that promote the rights and interests of workers, held tremendous amount of influence over the American economy in the first half of the 20th century. In 1954 one in every three workers was unionized. Today that number has fallen, and only 15 percent of all American workers are members of a union.

In the last 100 years, the three types of people involved in businesses—owners, manager, and workers—have gotten all mixed up. Now, it's not uncommon to find employee-owned companies, in which workers actually team up and buy the company they work for. Labor unions, while they don't risk their own capital, have been able to affect how companies are run. By joining together and acting as one unit instead of hundreds or thousands of individuals, labor unions can exert influence over owners and managers that an individual could not.

Companies rarely produce anything all by themselves. Usually a product is the result of several—sometimes several dozen—different companies that each produce a part of the product.

For example, newspapers arrive on millions of doorsteps every morning. But every newspaper is possible only because of the efforts of thousands of different people—owners, managers and workers—and lots of different companies.

One company makes the paper the news is printed on. Another company ships the paper to the newspaper printing offices. The newspaper owners themselves put up all the money each day to buy the paper, betting that they will sell enough advertisements and newspapers the next day to make money. The reporters and editors find out all the information that goes into a newspaper. Sometimes, there's yet another company that ships the printed newspapers to the deliverymen and women. Deliverymen and women usually work for themselves, and the newspaper pays them a fee to make sure the newspaper arrives on everyone's doorstep.

This same story can be told for all kinds of products. Cars are made up of thousands of parts made by many different companies. Video games, computers, school desks, the school you go to each day, are made by different people and companies all working together to create a finished product. Each in its turn was paid for the work or the piece of the product it made. The workers were paid their wages, the managers were paid their salaries and bonuses for making sure the product was made properly and on time, and the owners took home the profit from the sale.

Over the years, a system of methods for conducting a business have evolved, covering such things as how long a company should take to pay a supplier, how often to pay employees, and providing safe working conditions. Some of these matters are covered by laws and some of them by unwritten customs.

Business customs are rules that have to do with history, culture, and etiquette. For instance, many companies require their employees to dress a certain way. It's customary for business owners and managers to set rules about business dress. Similarly, it's customary to pay suppliers within 30 days. It's proper etiquette to treat competitors, employees,

Women in the Workforce

Just 40 years ago women made up a very small portion of the total workforce in the United States and rarely became managers. It was a man's world. Today women make up over 45 percent of all management positions in companies. In high-paying fields, such as law and medicine, however, only about one in every three professionals are women.

In 1999, 11 European countries created a single kind of currency, called the euro, to make it easier to do business between their countries. Each country's coin had its own design. The above are the backs of the German euros, which became the country's official currency on January 1, 2002.

and business associates with respect and decency. While there are laws against cheating someone, it's very bad form for companies to cheat a customer, and companies that do so usually damage their reputation. And a company's good reputation is one of its most prized possessions, because it's usually something that can't be bought, but only built up over time through good business practices.

Laws also exist that govern how companies and businesses behave toward each other, their customers, and their workers. These kinds of laws are called **regulations.** Virtually every industry has a government agency, known as a regulator, which oversees practices within that industry to ensure businesses don't harm the public through bad or unsafe business practices. Banks, candy makers, the electric company, the hospital—all of them have regulators that issue rules for how they do business. If companies don't follow these rules, the government can shut them down or punish the owners and managers with fines or jail time.

In a capitalist system the goal of a business is to make a profit. There is an old saying that says "money makes the world go 'round." More to the point, money makes business happen. It's like the grease in the bicycle wheel of the economy. Without money, it would be a lot harder to make the economy work.

Money in some form has been around for thousands of years. Some historians say that money was first invented 4000 years ago when early civilization used different types of metal as a uniform way of exchange. Anything can serve as money. Through history, different civilizations used all kinds of things for money. American Indians used beads made from shells. The early European settlers to America used tobacco as money. In Germany after World War II, there was no German currency so people used cigarettes and liquor to buy things. The people of the Pacific island of Yap used stone disks as money, some of them weighing hundreds of pounds.

Every big economy needs a method of exchange, or a way that everyone agrees is the best way to buy and sell things. That's why the European Union countries decided to create a new, uniform currency in 1999. To facilitate trade, they decided 1 currency would be much easier than 11 different ones. The European Union countries began phasing out their individual currencies and using a new kind of money, called the euro. Money is much more than paper and coins, it's the one thing that everyone agrees is worth something. And it's only worth something because we all say it is.

With money, everything can be assigned a value that everyone understands. For instance, a box of breakfast cereal may cost $2.50. Using money to put a value on the box of cereal, most people with a basic understanding of the American dollar can understand how much that box of cereal is worth. But what if we were to say the box of cereal costs two skateboard wheels or half a box of crayons? How much is that worth? The world uses money because it is like a language that we can all understand when we do business.

The dollar is important to our economy because it is a unit of money whose value everyone agrees upon. The government strictly controls almost everything about the dollar, from where and how it is printed, where it is stored, and how much of it is in circulation. The **Federal Reserve** is a series of large, government banks that helps control the supply of money and, in that way, helps keep prices of everything relatively stable. This is why the federal government alone can print dollars. A sign that money isn't doing its job very well is when the prices of all goods go up fast. This is called **inflation**.

Using money, large amounts of wealth and capital can be moved around relatively easily. America has thousands of banks that hold onto people's savings and make loans to

Borrowing

Borrowing has been a fact of life since the beginning of civilization. Economists call borrowed money debt. Most people, for example, can't afford to buy a home without borrowing some of the money. Americans borrow more money than any other people on earth. Household debt in the United States is currently at an all-time high, and almost every American has a credit card. But personal bankruptcies are also at all-time highs: 1.3 million people filed for bankruptcy in the United States in 1997.

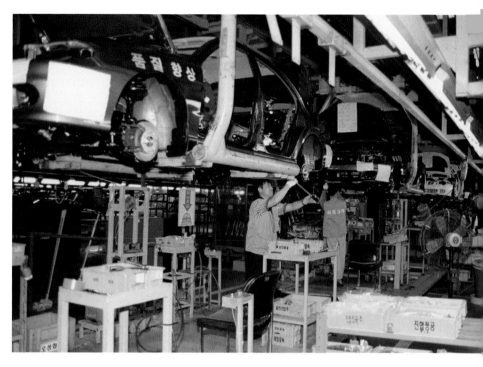

Assembly line workers piece cars together at a Hyundai Motors plant in South Korea. Invented by Henry Ford in the early 20th century, the assembly line is still used in manufacturing today.

people to buy things like cars and houses. People who want to buy a business sometimes go to a bank to borrow the money for it. Banks charge a certain portion of the amount being borrowed, called interest, and it and the loan amount is paid back over an agreed-upon period of time. This is called **financing,** and it's an important part of how business gets done. Without the ability to borrow money and pay it back over time, all the wealth would stay in one place: in the bank.

The idea of risk is a basic factor in a free market. To take a risk, you have to have something to risk. In business, often what you risk is money—sometimes a lot of it. But not any one person or company has all the money needed

A man asks a question during a stockholders meeting. Stockholders are the owners of a company, and they have a say in how the company is run.

in a big enterprise. For instance, General Motors, the biggest carmaker in the world and the maker of the Corvette, GMC trucks, the Camaro, and dozens of other types of cars, needs billions and billions of dollars to make all those cars. Since no one person has that much money to risk, General Motors risks money that comes from many sources.

General Motors risks money that its own **stockholders** have invested in the company. Stockholders are the owners, each owning a small portion of the company in the form of stock. General Motors has millions of individual stockholders. Stocks are bought and sold like any other product, which is good for General Motors because it can sell more of its stock if it needs to raise more money to build more cars.

The General Motors corporation may borrow money from banks directly, but big companies don't usually borrow from banks. Smaller companies, however, borrow from banks all the time to expand their business. Larger companies often borrow money by selling **bonds.** Bonds are like a loan that is broken up in many tiny pieces and sold to **investors.**

If an investor buys a 1-year bond with a face value of $1,000 and earns interest on it at a rate of 10 percent a year, at the end of the year he would have $1,100. The total interest earned on the bond for the year would be $100. Bonds are attractive investments, and they help large companies and municipalities to pay for their operations and to expand.

A long line of homeless and jobless men wait outside in the cold for a free meal at New York's municipal lodging house in the winter of 1932–33. In the years following the stock market crash of 1929, bank failures wiped out the savings of millions of Americans, and businesses closed, putting them out of work.

Business Cycles

What goes up must come down. That's not only true of baseballs and balloons, but of the economy as well. The word economy can mean a lot of different things, but generally it means the overall commercial health of a country. A good economy means people have good jobs and more jobs are being created all the time. A good economy means that there is plenty of money for people and businesses to borrow. Businesspeople feel safe taking the kinds of risks that can lead to innovation and bigger profits.

Most people don't notice when there's a good economy. An economist once said that no one would recognize that there even was an economy unless the economy sometimes didn't work so well. But, jokes aside, a healthy economy is important for business. It makes it easier for people to have good jobs with high pay. It also gives people job security, so they don't have to worry about being fired or laid off when the companies they work for don't sell enough of their products. A healthy economy can mean more money for you to buy books and music, and it can mean better schools and parks in your neighborhood.

A lot of things can cause a bad economy, and it's usually a combination of things that forces an economy to get sick. In the 1920s, the American economy was growing and lots of people had more money than they ever had before. It led people to **speculate,** or bet their own money that the economy would continue to grow and be very healthy. Usually, people speculated in the stocks of companies. The stock market went up and up and up until 1929, when it crashed. It was the shock of that crash, combined with all kinds of problems the world was having at the time, which led to a decade known as the **Great Depression.**

During the Great Depression, everything became worth a lot less money than it had just a few years earlier. That caused people to lose everything they owned, and banks to fail. Many other businesses failed, too. By 1932, almost one out of every three adults didn't have a job. Businesses produced about half of what they had produced in 1929.

The Depression lasted for 10 years, and during that time many people in the United States and the world were very poor. These economic problems led to a lot of other problems, too. European countries experienced political and social turmoil, which eventually led to World War II.

In 1932 the Depression had gotten so bad that it changed the way the U.S. government interacted with people and

At one time industrial cities in America were clouded in smoke from coal-burning factories and steel mills. The smoke has mostly cleared, but these factories built America into an industrial giant that today represents about 22 percent of the entire world economy.

businesses forever. From that point forward, the government would take a much more active role in governing not just people, but the economy as well. The federal government became involved in banks, businesses, and farming. President Franklin Delano Roosevelt used government money and resources to slowly take the country out of the Depression. He came up with a package of programs to improve the economy and people's lives during these troubled economic times. Called the New Deal, these programs used the vast resources of the federal government to employ out-of-work people. He also created an insurance system for banks so that, if banks failed, people wouldn't lose their savings. Roosevelt's programs greatly expanded the role of government in the economy and in society. While he is credited with helping the country out of the Great Depression, many people thought then and still think today that Roosevelt's policies made government much too big for a free society.

It wasn't until World War II ended in 1945 that America really recovered from the Depression. Since then, the economy has been very healthy, with few exceptions. America wasn't damaged in the war the way many other countries were. New systems were put in place to regulate stocks, banks, production, and money that have helped keep the "ups" of the business cycle from being so big that the "downs" don't hurt too badly. After World War II, the United States became the biggest and strongest economy in the world.

The Big Mac Index

To help compare the spending power of people in different countries, economists came up with "The Big Mac Index." Invented by the London-based magazine *The Economist,* the index uses a Big Mac from McDonald's as a standard way to price the value of different currencies. A McDonald's hamburger is made nearly the same the world over, so it's a good way to compare the buying power of different currencies against the dollar. If the Big Mac Index of a country goes up faster than it does in other countries, it's a sign that country's currency is getting out of whack. A banker came up with a way to relate it to different people's incomes in different countries. In 1997 it took people in Venezuela almost two hours to earn enough money to buy a Big Mac. In Tokyo, Japan, it took the average person just nine minutes to earn enough to buy a Big Mac.

Today, we still see shocks like the stock market crash of 1929. For instance, in 1987 the dollar value of the stock market fell even further in two days than it did in 1929. Many economists worried that it would trigger a **recession.** But it didn't. In fact, between 1987 and 2000, the American economy became healthier and grew faster than it had in the previous 30 years. Many economists believe that the government and business systems set up after the Great Depression prevented the 1987 stock market crash from causing a bigger economic collapse. Those safeguards include the Federal Reserve, a system of government banks that helps control the supply of money in circulation. The Federal Reserve helps keep prices from going up or down too fast. If prices go up fast, it's known as inflation, and as we mentioned earlier, inflation is one of the key indicators of a sick economy.

As of 2001, the chairman of the Federal Reserve was Alan Greenspan, whom many business people call the second most powerful person in the world, second only to the President of the United States. Greenspan is an economist who helps set monetary policy, which is the attitude of the Federal Reserve toward the money supply and interest rates. Greenspan was a boy during the Great Depression, and he witnessed firsthand many of America's great economic ups and downs. He was appointed Chairman of the Federal Reserve in 1987, and is credited with creating a monetary policy that helped the economy recover from the stock market crash of 1987 and become one of the healthiest economies in the history of the country. A congressman once said of Greenspan, "He is the kind of person who knows how many thousands of flat-headed bolts were used in a Chevrolet and what it would do to the national economy if you took out three of them."

A technician cleans a Sewer Access Module robot after it installed commercial fiberoptic cable through the sewer system in Albuquerque, New Mexico, in March 2001. Robots are one of many new kinds of technology that have helped the economy grow in recent years.

In addition to the Federal Reserve, another thing that keeps shocks from spreading out of control is the simple idea of economic diversity. The United States has so many different kinds of industries and so many people engaged in different enterprises, that if one of them should collapse, the others aren't always affected so badly. California may be having economic problems, but people across the country in New York might not even notice it.

But the world is a big place, and the economy of the United States is linked with all of it. Global trade, or the practice of nations buying and selling products among each other, has grown very large in the last 20 years. America, isn't as isolated as it once was, and economic problems in China, or Japan, or Russia will affect the economy in the United States.

In the 1990s, things began happening in the economy that couldn't be explained using history as a guide. Economic growth surged, and the stock market quadrupled in value as a **bull market** took hold that beat all others in history combined. In many parts of the country, there weren't enough workers to fill all the job openings, and personal income in real terms rose for the first time in decades. Consumer spending on things like cars, stereos, and video games increased dramatically.

But production, measured by the amount of goods produced in places like factories, did not increase as fast. To

Brand Recognition

What is a brand? In the New Economy, the concept of branding became important to information companies. At a time when information is very hard to control—e-mail can beam an idea to millions of people in a few minutes—brands are how companies differentiate their product. For instance, America Online is the world's most successful Internet company. It provides access to the Internet using telephone lines. Hundreds of companies offer the exact same service. But America Online created such a powerful brand that people, often without thinking about it, believe America Online is the best option to get hooked up to the Internet. Of course, America Online has worked very hard and invested billions of dollars to make its brand the best, by adding services and improving its customer service. But the creation of America Online as a great brand, and not necessarily a great Internet company, is its most profitable accomplishment.

explain the fast-growing economy of the 1990s, economists and prominent business people came up with the idea of the **New Economy,** where old rules about production, wealth creation, and the flow of capital no longer apply. The New Economy was based on several factors: globalization, the importance of information and knowledge, and technology.

In 1992 the United States, Canada, and Mexico, the three countries that make up the North American continent, agreed to the **North American Free Trade Agreement (NAFTA).** NAFTA made it possible for goods to move across the borders of these three countries more cheaply and easily by gradually eliminating the fees companies had to pay to sell their products in other countries.

NAFTA ushered in a decade in which global trade grew on an unprecedented scale, and the economies of the world all began to interact in ways they never had. Countries in Europe formed the European Union, in which their economies became one.

Economists call this trend **globalization,** and it has far-reaching consequences for people everywhere. The more economies in different countries become linked, the more everyone is affected by what goes on in the rest of the world. For instance, if China should go into a long economic decline, it would affect much of the rest of the world. Under NAFTA, if Mexico's economy improves, the United States will benefit.

In the last 10 years, the information and media industries have become bigger and more powerful. People make money off ideas, now, in ways that they never have before. In legal terms, this is called **intellectual property,** and it refers to everything from ideas for movies, to computer programming, to music. Intellectual property can be mass-produced at very little cost. For instance, a song is written

Microsoft founder Bill Gates has benefitted from the sale of his Windows computer software, considered intellectual property, which the company licenses to computer users around the world.

and recorded once, but the real money comes from reproducing an album many times over and selling it. The ability to control and move intellectual property has made some of the great fortunes of the New Economy.

For example, Bill Gates formed Microsoft to sell a computer program that he created. It was called DOS, and it helped personal computers run. DOS didn't take much to produce. It cost just pennies to copy it onto different computers. But the Microsoft Corporation owns and controls the rights to DOS, and as it became more popular with computer users in the 1980s, Microsoft and Gates made billions of dollars licensing DOS to computer makers.

Today Microsoft is one of the most valuable companies on the planet, and much of the wealth is based on the ideas of Bill Gates. In that way, Gates is very different from someone like Henry Ford. Gates thought up an entirely new product that had no moving parts, whereas Ford invented new ways of manufacturing things. Gates's product doesn't take that much to make; Ford's product took whole factories full of people to make. In today's economy, ideas can make more money than making cars.

The last piece to the New Economy puzzle is technology. Technology, particularly computer technology and communications technology, has taken such huge leaps in the last 10 years that many economists believe it has made it possible to improve the economy without many of the costs associated with fast growth. For instance, in past periods of fast economic growth, society has had to bear the burdens of high population growth and environmental problems from pollution, to cite just two examples.

But with advancements in technology, production can grow much more efficiently. Computers can hold and process nearly infinite amounts of information, helping business managers make decisions about when to buy supplies. Communications have improved so much that even managers at a big, multinational company like General Motors can have information about all the company's operations almost instantly. This can help them to operate the business more efficiently.

Today, workers are using tools unheard of 10 years ago to make more products in less time. Manufacturing has become automated, and robots now make pieces of cars that used to take dozens of people. Better technology has made better steel, better plastics, better sound on your CDs, better graphics on your video games, better reception for your television, and much of it is done with fewer people than it was when your father and mother were little.

All of these trends—globalization, information, and technology—combined were major factors in the economic growth of the 1990s. Many economists believe the New Economy not only helped the economy grow faster, but also helped distribute wealth to places and people much easier and more fairly. And to many people who became rich in technology and in the stock market, "old rules don't apply" became a rallying cry to a better way of life.

But for all the good things that happened in the 1990s, the 21st century dawned and most of the world's most pressing economic problems had not disappeared. Wealth was created, but most of it was created for very few people. The problems of poverty, education, and health care in the United States persisted, and in some cities grew worse.

Globalization brought down economic barriers between countries, but many countries' economic and political systems did not improve the health and welfare of their people. The African continent, for instance, continues to suffer widespread political and social problems, and the economies of many African countries are in ruins.

By 2000 the powerful economy in the United States showed signs that the old rules did apply. The stock market, after quadrupling in value in the 1990s, began losing value, and by the spring of 2001 it had lost most of the gains of the last five years. Internet companies and other businesses, whose success relied on more and more people adopting new technology, began to fail. The World Wide Web had indeed changed the way people get information and communicate, but only a handful of companies had made money from it.

A Chinese man looks at bundles of scallions at a street market in Beijing. China has taken steps to introduce free market principles into its economy, such as allowing people to own small businesses.

Different Types of Economies

A free market economy is one in which individuals and companies make individual choices, without the control of the government or other central authority. That's where the word "free" in free market comes from: people are free to make their own economic decisions about what to buy and sell and for how much.

Not every country lives under this system. The world's economic system is really made up of countless small economic systems, of which the United States is only a part. People with different histories, political systems, and cultures design other systems.

Berliners celebrate the November 1989 tearing down of the wall that had separated East and West Germany. West Germany, under a free market system, had prospered; East Germany, under a Communist system, was poor and underdeveloped. Once they combined under freedom, they built a strong economy.

At the opposite end of the economic spectrum is the command economy, in which one central authority, usually the government, makes most economic decisions. In a command economy, the public owns most factories and companies, and the government decides what each factory and company will make, how much it will make, and at what price it will be sold. Often, these government decisions are made from a political standpoint, and this central planning of the economy is used to accomplish social and cultural goals.

One type of command economy is called **communism.** Communism is an economic system that advocates the elimination of private property. In its ideal form, it is a system in which goods are owned in common and are distributed on an as-needed basis. In real life examples, such as in the former Soviet Union, communism has been a totalitarian form of government in which a small group of people have controlled the state-owned means of production while the majority of people have had no authority. The communists believe that all of life is a class struggle between the workers and the owners of the means of production, such as the owners of a factory.

Unfortunately, this struggle led to decades of war and political strife in much of the world in the 20th century. Working out the differences between communism and the free market economy continues today, mostly without war. Different countries have different ideas about what makes a good economy.

Political Instability and a Poor Economy

Comoros is considered one of the poorest countries in the world. Located on a chain of very small islands in the Indian Ocean off the coast of South Africa, the half-million people who live there are mostly farmers and ranchers who grow their own food. There are hardly any stores or paved roads. What factories they have are used to make agricultural products, such as food oils and spices, to sell to other countries. Even so, Comoros does not provide enough food to feed its own people, and unemployment is very high. This economic trouble has gone hand-in-hand with political trouble: there have been 18 military revolutions or attempts to overthrow the government on Comoros since 1975.

For communists, central planning is essential to their political goal of elevating the worker to the status of owner, and vice versa. In a command economy, rules like risk and supply-and-demand don't have the same effect as they do in a free market economy. In a command economy, just because there's a lot of demand for bubble gum doesn't mean that more bubble gum gets made, and it certainly doesn't mean that bubble gum will be expensive. The state might decide, for example, that bubble gum is bad for people's teeth, and stop making it altogether. Or to control the price of bubble gum, it might subsidize—or help pay for—the costs of making gum.

The communists called the goals of a centrally planned economy **socialism.** The biggest and most famous socialist state in history was the Union of Soviet Socialist Republics, (U.S.S.R.). The Soviet socialist regime lasted from 1918 to 1989. They used a command economy to minimize the difference between the rich and the poor. They also used their

Adam Smith

Adam Smith was the first philosopher who took a starkly economic view of the world and its people. Smith, a Scotsman who lived in the 1700s, wrote *The Wealth of Nations*, which remains the basis for nearly all economic theory today. To Smith, humans were self-interested, but also able to feel sympathy and compassion. The combination of these qualities led each person, without even intending it, to advance and improve society by their own self-interested decisions. He called this process "the invisible hand" of the economy. In Smith's view, all of us are guided by this invisible hand when we make cost-benefit decisions, purchases, or business decisions.

Russians in Moscow line up at an outdoor market to buy dairy products in 1999. The Communist system, in which the state had owned all the farms and factories, never produced enough of anything to meet consumers' needs. Long lines of people hoping to buy whatever they can find remain common.

centrally planned economy to mobilize the entire country during national emergencies and wars. One of the reasons the Soviets were on the winning side during World War II was because the government, using its all-encompassing authority, could keep the country and every factory and person in it focused on winning, no matter what the cost.

But a command economy has many drawbacks, and ultimately has been unsuccessful as a model for how to run an economic system. First of all, running an entire economy from one place is incredibly complex. A central planner's inability to find and predict problems of supply and demand usually leads to inefficiency, or the inability of an economy to perform at its optimum level. For the Soviets, the result was that most people were relatively poor. Central planning also led to corruption and, ultimately, political strife. The U.S.S.R broke up in the late 1980s. Today, while it still has many political and social problems, Russia has moved toward a free-market economy.

But socialism, as an idea, continues to guide many economic systems. Even though it has a free market economy, the United States has several programs that are socialist in nature. The Social Security System is a centrally run government program to provide income and services to the old and weak. The Medicare and Medicaid programs use tax dollars to provide medical benefits to those in need. Governmental authorities regulate large parts of some industries, such as the electric power industry and the banking industry.

In fact, most countries in the world today have large, state-owned enterprises. Governments may own banking systems, automobile manufacturers, gasoline companies, and airlines.

The People's Republic of China, with over three billion people, is the largest centrally planned economy in the world, and its rulers are still guided by communist principles of a single economic and political authority. In recent years, however, even China has taken steps to introduce free market principles into its communist society. Chinese citizens can now own property, open businesses, and profit from their investments.

What is happening in China is one example of the changes that take place in all of the world's economies over time. Every economic system is continuously evolving.

Even the new economies of the Information Age, fueled by technology and globalization, might turn out to be just another phase in the history of economics. In the 1800s, the Industrial Revolution turned England and America into powerful, wealthy nations with large cities, sprawling factories, and huge industrial companies. In the process, it changed everything about how people lived. Only time will tell if the New Economy will have that kind of impact on the world.

Bankruptcy—when a company or a person runs out of money to pay their bills, they seek protection under the United States Bankruptcy Code

Bear market—when most investors believe the stock market will go down

Bond—companies sell bonds to investors to raise money; the company promises to pay back the bond, plus interest

Bull market—a period in which investors believe the stock market will go higher

Capital—money that is needed to set up and operate a business

Capitalism—an economic system characterized by private ownership of capital

Command economy—an economy that is controlled from a central authority, usually the government

Communism—an economic system advocating the elimination of private property so that all goods may be owned in common and available to all on an as-needed basis

Consumer—one who spends money buying goods or services

Consumer spending—the amount of money not used in basic living expenses spent by individuals on things like movies, restaurants, video games and Christmas gifts

Division of labor—the practice of letting different workers work on specific parts of a product

Dow Jones Industrial Average (Dow)—the most widely watch stock index, it is one indicator of how well the stock market is doing

Economics—the study of the economy

Economy—any system in which a method of exchange exists to trade products and services

Entrepreneur—a person, sometimes an inventor, who builds a business from scratch

Exchange—any way individuals have for recognizing the value of products; in the United States, the dollar is the most recognizable method of exchange

Federal Reserve System—the system of federal banks that controls the money supply and helps set interest rates

Financing—the process of borrowing money to build a business

Free market—the idea that people are free to make up their minds about where to spend and invest their money

Globalization—term used to describe the growing economic links between countries around the world

Great Depression—a period during the 1930s in which the American economy was in severe decline, leading to widespread poverty and unemployment

Inflation—a period during which prices of goods and services rise quickly

Intellectual Property—ownership of an idea

Internet—a network of computers that an individual with a personal computer can tap into to view information around the world

Investors—Individuals and investment companies that buy stocks and bonds

Labor union—a group of individuals that group together to demand better pay and working conditions

New Economy—a term used to describe how technology and globalization are making companies more efficient and wealth easier to obtain

North American Free Trade Agreement (NAFTA)—an agreement between Canada, the United States, and Mexico to eliminate trade barriers

Recession—a period of slow or no growth in the economy

Regulations—rules and standards that governments set to control business and industry

Socialism—a system of living in which there is no private property and the means of production oare owned and controlled by the state

Speculate—to bet money on a risky proposition hoping to make money

Standard of living—term used to describe how well individuals and families live in any given economy

Stockholder—a person who owns or buys stocks

Supply and demand—one of the basic rules of economics, the rule of supply and demand says that the prices of products are set by supply working in relation to demand, and vice versa; for example, when demand is high, the supply declines, and prices go up

Wages—the amount of money individuals get paid to work at their job; sometimes this amount is also called a salary

Andryszewski, Tricia. *The Environment and the Economy: Planting the Seeds for Tomorrow's Growth.* Millbrook, 1995.

Burgess, John. *World Trade.* Philadelphia: Chelsea House Publishers, 2002.

Downes, John, and Jordan Elliot Goodman. *Dictionary of Finance and Investment Terms.* New York: Barron's Educational Series, 1998

Geisst, William R., *Wall Street: A History.* Oxford University Press, Oxford, England, 1999.

Heintz, James, and Nancy Folbre. *The Ultimate Field Guide to the U.S. Economy: A Compact and Irreverent Guide to Economic Life in America.* New York: The New Press, 2000.

MacKay, Charles, and Andrew Tobias. *Extraordinary Popular Delusions & the Madness of Crowds.* New York: Crown Publishing, 1995.

Otfinoski, Steve. *The Kids Guide to Money: Earning It, Saving It, Spending It, Growing It, Sharing It.* New York: Scholastic, 1996.

Reeves, Diane Lindsey. *Career Ideas for Kids Who Like Money.* New York: Facts On File, 2001.

Sowell, Thomas. *Basic Economics: A Citizen's Guide to the Economy.* New York: Basic Books, 2000.

Picture Credits

TERENCE O'HARA is a writer and business editor at *The Washington Post*. He lives in Baltimore.